Where We Live

Brazil

Donna Bailey and Anna Sproule

STECK-VAUGHN
LIBRARY
A Division of Steck-Vaughn Company

Hello! My name is Gilberto,
and this is my friend Pedro.
We live in Rio de Janeiro, Brazil.
Pedro and I are taking care of
Dad's vegetable stand.

2

Rio de Janeiro is a city by the sea.

The mountains come right down to the water.

The big pointed mountain in this picture

is called Sugar Loaf Mountain.

Tourists like to ride up to the top
of Sugar Loaf Mountain in cable cars.
There is a good view of the bays and
beaches around Rio from the mountain top.

We used to live in the country,
but Dad came to Rio to find a job.
He found a piece of land near
the edge of town and built a house.
Our house is on the side of a mountain.

Many families live on the mountain.
There are steps up to
the different levels.
My friends and I have races
up and down the steps.

We like to play soccer on
a flat piece of ground or on a street
farther down the mountain.

These are my brothers Antonio and Jorge
and my sisters Ireina and Maria.
Our dog had three puppies.
I think Antonio wants to hold
one of the puppies, too!

Mom works as a cook for
a family who lives in town.
Here she is, cooking in their kitchen.
She often makes black beans for them.
Black beans with rice is
my favorite food.

My sister Tereza is a nanny and takes care of
the two youngest children of the family.
Sometimes Tereza takes the children
to the park to swing.

Tereza also takes the children
to Copacabana Beach.
They like to go early in the morning
before it gets too hot.

The beach gets very crowded in the afternoon.
People go there to swim and sunbathe.

There's always a group of boys
playing soccer on the beach.
Everyone in Brazil likes soccer!

The players get very hot after their game,
so they buy soft drinks
from the boys on the beach.
The ice helps keep the drinks cool.

People also buy big, juicy slices of
watermelons in the nearby market.

This woman sells watermelons and
other kinds of fruit on the beach.
She sells avocados, little bananas,
coconuts, and big pineapples.

The beaches are always clean.
Workers walk along the beach all day,
picking up trash and empty cans.
Children can play safely on the sand.
They won't cut their feet on glass or cans.

On New Year's Eve in Rio de Janeiro,
crowds of people go to the beach.
The women wear white dresses and
carry flowers, candles, and little statues.

18

The girls each decorate the beach
with flowers and candles.

Then they light the candles and
wait for the tide to come in.
If the sea carries their gifts away,
it means they will have good luck
in the coming year.

20

Sometimes the girls can't wait
for the tide to come in.
They run into the water and
throw their flowers into the sea.

Afterward, there is a huge feast
of tasty snacks and tortillas.
A tortilla is a kind of pancake with
different fillings.

Everyone buys fireworks
and many people have
fireworks parties.

The children dress up in
country-style clothes.
They paint their faces
with burned cork.

In the evening, everyone sets off
their fireworks.
Even the little children stay up and
enjoy the fireworks and sparklers.
Brazilians say the noise of the fireworks
wakes Saint John from his sleep.

Then everyone joins in the feast.

There are always good things to eat.

The roasted ears of corn are
a special treat for everybody!

The feasting and dancing
last well into the night.
Everyone enjoys the fun of
Saint John's festival.

Index

Reading Consultant: Diana Bentley
Editorial Consultant: Donna Bailey
Executive Editor: Elizabeth Strauss
Project Editor: Becky Ward

Picture research by Jennifer Garratt
Designed by Richard Garratt Design

Photographs
Cover: Stephanie Colasanti FBIPP
Colorific Photo Library: 7,13 (Claus Neyer), 16 (Ciro Mariano), 18,19,20 (Walter Firmo)
Brazil Photo Library: 4,5,6,9,10,11,15,21,22,26,27,28,29,30,31,32 (Lupe Cunha)
The Hutchison Library: 3,24 (Michael MacIntire), 14,25 (Cavan McCarthy), 2,8,23
Robert Harding Picture Library: title page, 12,17

Library of Congress Cataloging-in-Publication Data: Bailey, Donna. Brazil / Donna Bailey and Anna Sproule.
p. cm.—(Where we live)   ISBN 0-8114-2560-6   1. Brazil—Social life and customs—Juvenile literature.
I. Sproule, Anna. II. Title. III. Series: Bailey, Donna. Where we live. F2510.B22 1990 981′.53063—
dc20 90-30534 CIP AC